DISASTERS

TERRORISM

ANN WEIL

SADDLEBACK
EDUCATIONAL PUBLISHING

DISASTERS

SADDLEBACK
EDUCATIONAL PUBLISHING
www.sdlback.com

ISBN-13: 978-1-61651-936-0
ISBN-10: 1-61651-936-3
eBook: 978-1-61247-632-2

Printed in Malaysia

21 20 19 18 17   4 5 6 7 8

Photo Credits: cover, NewsCom; pages 14, 23, Bettmann/Corbis; page
31, Peter Turnley/Corbis; page 43, Reuters NewMedia/Corbis; page 61,
BlackStar Photos; page 67, © Alvaro Ennes | Dreamstime.com; pages
74–75, © Andrew Chambers | Dreamstime.com; page 88, © Maggern |
Dreamstime.com

CONTENTS

DATAFILE

Timeline

April 18, 1983

Bomb explodes at the US Embassy in Beirut.

October 23, 1983

Bomb explodes at US Marine Barracks in Beirut.

Where is Beirut?

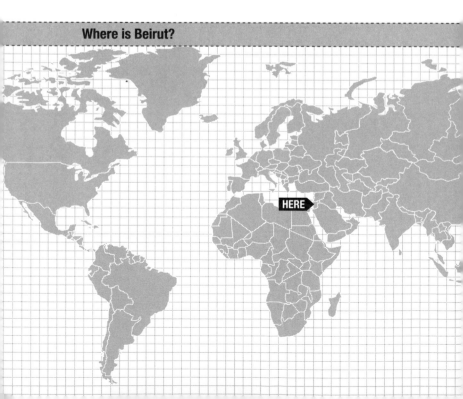

Key Terms

hijack—to take control of a car, bus, plane, or train, etc., by force

hostage—a person held against his or her will by a terrorist

terrorism—using force or threats against people

CHAPTER 1 | Introduction

Some disasters happen by accident. But terrorists destroy things on purpose. And that's when loss of life is most cruel.

Thousands died in terror attacks on the World Trade Center and the Pentagon on September 11, 2001. It was the deadliest terror disaster in history.

What is terrorism?

Terrorism is violence against normal people. It is not the same as war. Terrorists do not belong to a country's armed forces. They don't often act for any one country.

Most terror groups are small. Only a few people may be involved in any one attack. They hijack planes. They hold people hostage. They threaten to kill hostages, and sometimes do.

They explode bombs. They destroy property and kill people. Many times, families and children are the victims.

Terror groups want to scare people. They do this to get power. Sometimes they have a goal in mind. They may want to free others who are in prison.

Some think that they are helping others by killing. They call themselves "freedom fighters." They say they are fighting for freedom. But they are spreading pain.

The United States and others around the world are working to stop terror so people can live in peace and without fear of attack.

DATAFILE

Timeline

September 5, 1972

Terrorists kill 11 Israeli athletes at the Olympic Games in Munich.

November 1972

Richard M. Nixon, 37th president of the United States, is elected to serve a second term.

Where is Munich?

HERE ▶

Key Terms

grenade—a small bomb often thrown by hand

mastermind—a clever person who plans and directs a group project

Palestinians—citizens of Palestine, a region west of the Jordan River at the eastern end of the Mediterranean Sea. Palestine existed as a British mandated territory from 1917 until Israel was founded in 1948.

CHAPTER 2 | The Munich Massacre, 1972

The Olympic Games stand for good will among all people and nations. Millions watch the games on TV. People enjoy seeing athletes from all over the world compete.

But the 1972 games were different. The TV image many recall is not of an athlete with a gold medal. It is of a terrorist in a ski mask with a gun.

September 5, 1972

At about 4:30 a.m., five men climbed a fence into the Olympic Village. Three more men were already inside. They knocked on the door of Israel's wrestling coach. When the door opened, they rushed in.

The wrestling coach and a weightlifter tried to block the door. This helped others to escape. But the two brave men were killed.

Nine Israelis were taken hostage. The men who took the athletes said that they were Palestinians. They demanded that Israel release more than 200 Arabs from prison.

They said they would kill the Israeli athletes if their demand was not met. The men also wanted a plane to fly them out of Germany.

Many tense hours passed. Then, it was agreed that a bus would take the men and hostages to a helicopter. The helicopter would fly them to an air base. A plane would be waiting. The plane would fly everyone to Cairo, Egypt.

But the German police had another plan. They thought they might be able to shoot the terrorists at the airport.

There was a bloody gun battle. They killed the five terrorists who had jumped the fence. However, they didn't know that there were really eight.

At first, people thought the hostages were safe. But the news reports were too early. The hostages were still in the helicopters.

A terrorist pulled a grenade. He used it to blow up one of the helicopters. Another terrorist shot the hostages on the other helicopter. All were killed.

A German policeman died. The three terrorists who were left alive were captured.

The Games Go On

The next day, there was a special service for the 11 victims. The games were put off for one day.

Some thought the games should have been stopped. But the games went on.

The Terror Continues

Almost two months later, other terrorists hijacked a German airline jet. They demanded that the three terrorists in German prisons be set free. The Germans agreed.

Israeli agents were assigned to kill the terrorists. They also tracked down others who had helped plan the Munich attack. Most involved in the Munich Massacre are now dead. But the mastermind behind the terror is still free. He even wrote a book about it. In 1999, Abu Daoud published his story: *Memoirs of a Palestinian Terrorist.*

A member of the Olympic Committee speaks with a PLO (Palestine Liberation Organization) terrorist in the Olympic Village. The PLO took Olympic athletes as hostages and killed nine members of the Israeli Olympic Team at the 1972 Summer Games.

DATAFILE

Timeline

February 4, 1974

At age 19, Patty Hearst is taken from her Berkeley apartment by terrorists. She is the daughter of wealthy businessman Randolph Hearst.

January 1977

Jimmy Carter becomes the 39th president of the United States.

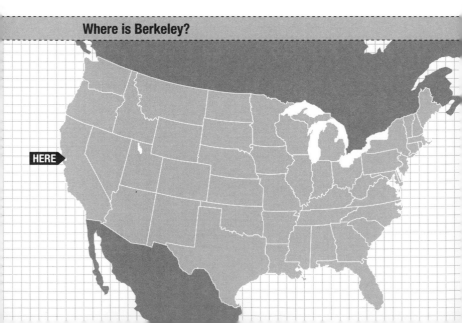

Where is Berkeley?

HERE

Did You Know?

The Symbionese Liberation Army (SLA) kidnapped Patty Hearst. Kathleen Soliah was an SLA member. Later, she ran and hid from justice. She used the name Sara Jane Olson.

Key Terms

brainwash—to change a person's beliefs by force

pardon—to free someone from further punishment

raid—a sudden hostile attack

CHAPTER 3 | Sara Jane Olson: A Secret Life

In the 1970s, Kathleen Soliah was part of an American terrorist group. They called themselves the Symbionese Liberation Army (SLA). The SLA was formed in 1973. It operated for only a few years.

Some SLA members were killed by police. Others were arrested. They went to jail. But the police did not catch Kathleen Soliah.

Kathleen escaped. She knew the police were looking for her. So she used a new name: Sara Jane Olson.

Years passed. Sara Jane Olson married. She had a family. She was a mother now, not a terrorist. Sara Jane Olson had left her past behind. But her past would not leave her.

In 1999, Sara Jane Olson was arrested. For 24 years, she had hidden her true name. Now, Sara Jane Olson was once again Kathleen Soliah. And she was in big trouble.

She was accused of planting bombs under police cars. In October 2001, Kathleen pleaded guilty to that charge. She was sentenced to 20 years to life in prison.

The Kidnapping of Patty Hearst

The SLA kidnapped Patty Hearst in 1974. Patty was 19 at the time. Patty's grandfather, William Randolph Hearst, was famous. He published newspapers and magazines. He was one of the richest men in America.

Everyone knew the Hearst fortune was worth many millions of dollars. The SLA forced the Hearst family to give two million dollars worth of food to the poor. But they did not let Patty go.

The SLA robbed a bank two months after the kidnapping. A hidden camera recorded the crime.

One of the bank robbers was Patty Hearst! She was carrying a machine gun. The newspapers printed a photo of Patty.

People wondered what had happened. Was Patty still a kidnapping victim? Or had she become a terrorist herself? No one really knew for sure.

The SLA made a videotape of Patty. On the tape, Patty said she had joined the SLA. She announced that her new name was Tania.

The police found out where the SLA members were hiding. More than 500 armed police raided the house. There was a shootout. The house burned to the ground.

Six SLA members died in the raid. Patty lived. She was arrested a year and a half later. Patty said that she was innocent. She pleaded not guilty at her trial.

She said the SLA had brainwashed her. She said they had locked her in a closet. They had tortured her. They had forced her to join the group.

Patty was found guilty. She was sentenced to seven years for armed robbery. But she was in jail for less than two years.

President Jimmy Carter shortened her sentence. Then, many years later, she received a pardon from President Bill Clinton.

SLA History

Marcus Foster

The SLA killed Marcus Foster in 1973. He was an educator who headed the Oakland, California, school system.

Two SLA members were arrested for the murder. Both were convicted.

Patty Hearst

The photo on page 23 convinced many people that Patty had really joined the SLA.

The SLA motto was, "Death to the fascist insect that preys upon the life of the people."

Patty Hearst said she was kidnapped and brainwashed by the SLA in 1974. Calling herself Tania, she was forced to participate in terrorist crimes of the SLA. This photo, released by the FBI, made many people believe she was no longer a kidnapping victim, but a member of the SLA.

The Murder of Myrna Lee Opsahl, 1975

The SLA robbed banks to support themselves. Myrna Lee Opsahl was shot dead during an SLA bank robbery. Mrs. Opsahl was a customer at the bank. She had four children. She was at the bank to deposit collection money from her church.

Where is Patty Hearst Today?

In 2000, Patty Hearst was in a John Water's film called *Cecil B. Demented*. She played the role of a young terrorist's mother.

Who was William Randolph Hearst?

Patty Hearst's grandfather was the publishing tycoon William Randolph Hearst (1863–1951), who built the largest newspaper chain in the United States. He and Joseph Pulitzer participated in a savage circulation competition in New York City, leading to the creation of yellow journalism— publishing stories for their sensationalism rather than for truth.

Hearst and his wife had five children, all boys. Although they never divorced, the couple maintained separate lives from the mid-1920s. From about 1919, Hearst carried on a decades-long affair with Hollywood actress Marion Davies, living with her openly.

Hearst built a castle on California's Central Coast, near San Simeon. It has 56 bedrooms, 61 bathrooms, 19 sitting rooms, 127 acres of gardens, swimming pools, tennis courts, and a movie theater. At the height of his power, Hearst owned 28 major newspapers, 18 magazines, plus several radio stations and movie companies.

DATAFILE

Timeline

January 1985

Ronald Reagan begins his second term as 40th president of the United States.

October 7, 1985

Vacationers on the cruise ship, *Achille Lauro*, are taken hostage in the Mediterranean Sea.

Where is the Mediterranean Sea?

HERE

Key Terms

government—a system of political control by which a nation is governed

parole—the freedom granted to a prisoner for future good behavior

Palestine Liberation Front—a Palestinian organization in Lebanon and Tunisia once headed by Abu Abbas

CHAPTER 4 | *Achille Lauro,* 1985

Hundreds of tourists were enjoying a cruise near Egypt. Then their nightmare began. Four terrorists took over the ship. They held everyone hostage.

The terrorists were part of a group called the Palestine Liberation Front. They wanted Israel to free 50 Palestinian prisoners. People around the world watched the horror unfold on television.

The terror went on for two days. Before it was over, an elderly American was murdered. Leon Klinghoffer was 69 years old. He was in a wheelchair.

The terrorists shot him because he was Jewish. Then they threw his body and the wheelchair over the side of the ship into the sea.

The Palestinian prisoners did not go free. Egypt offered the terrorists safety if they let the hostages go. So, the terrorists let the hostages go and gave themselves up.

The terrorists boarded an Egyptian jet. They thought they would escape. But American Navy fighter planes blocked their way.

They forced the Egyptian jet to land on the Italian island of Sicily. The terrorists were arrested in Italy.

Terrorists Go Free

The Italians were easy on the terrorists. One of the hijackers was granted parole in 1991. Two others disappeared after they left the prison. The American government was angry. The family of the murdered American protested.

Many people felt the terrorists should have stayed in jail. But there was little they could do. Other PLF members involved in the hijacking and murder are still at large.

In 2003, US troops captured the leader of the hijacking, Abu Abbas. They found him in Baghdad, Iraq.

The *Achille Lauro* in Port Said, after being hijacked by Palestinians for two days. The incident resulted in one death, Jewish American Leon Klinghoffer, who was shot and tossed overboard in his wheelchair.

DATAFILE

Timeline

May 26, 1978

A package bomb explodes at a university near Chicago. Over the next 17 years, many more bombs kill and injure others.

April 3, 1996

Theodore John Kaczynski is finally arrested in his Montana hideout.

Where is Montana?

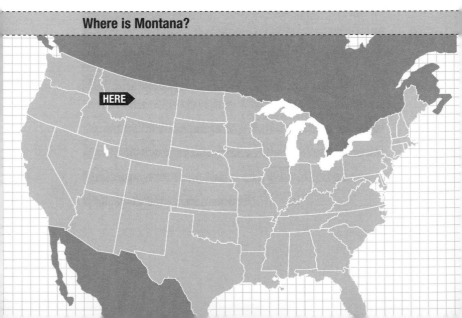

HERE

Key Terms

executive—a person who manages or administers a business or school, etc.

investigate—to search systematically in order to learn the facts

mathematics professor—a teacher of math at the college level

CHAPTER 5 | Unabomber

In May 1978, a package was found in a Chicago parking lot. The parking lot was at the University of Illinois. The package was sent from an address at another university near Chicago.

It was sent back. Someone there tried to open it. The package was really a bomb. It exploded. One person was hurt.

A terrorist had made the bomb. He left it in the parking lot. This was his first attack. But it was not his last.

Over the next seventeen years, he planted more bombs. Three people were killed. 23 more were wounded.

In April 1996, the FBI arrested Theodore John Kaczynski. Kaczynski was 53 years old. He was once a mathematics professor at a university in California. Now, people remember him as the Unabomber.

The Unabomber

The FBI investigated the 1978 bombing. But they could not trace the bomb back to anyone. About a year later, another bomb exploded at Northwestern University. Still, the FBI had no suspects.

Both bombs were made from scraps of wood and lamp cord and metal. At first, they called the case the "Junkyard Bomber."

Later, they noticed a pattern. Many of the victims were university professors. Others were airline executives. They began to call the case "Unabomb."

In December 1985, a bomb killed the owner of a computer store. The bomb was hidden inside a paper bag.

In 1987, a woman saw a man put a bag under the wheel of her car. She also worked at a computer store.

Another person who worked at the store tried to move the bag. It exploded. The person who tried to move the bag was badly hurt.

This time the FBI had a good lead. Someone had seen the Unabomber. A police artist drew a picture. This sketch was published in the newspapers.

The Unabomber looked like a white, middle-aged man with a mustache. He was wearing sunglasses and a sweatshirt with a hood.

Now everyone was looking for the Unabomber. But it would be many more years—and many more terrorist attacks—before he was stopped.

The Unabomber's Statement

In 1995, the Unabomber made an offer. He would stop his attacks if the newspapers printed something he had written. The newspapers agreed. They thought doing this would save lives.

The Unabomber's statement was published in September 1995. It was many pages long. It said that modern technology was destroying the human race.

Many people read the Unabomber's statement. One of them was David Kaczynski. He thought he knew the writing style.

It reminded him of letters his brother Ted had written. David Kaczynski got in touch with the FBI. He told them that his brother might be the Unabomber.

Theodore Kaczynski was arrested. He had been living in a one-room shack in Montana. The police found parts of a bomb there.

They also found early versions of the statement he had sent to the newspapers. There was even a diary that noted the bombings. The FBI had finally caught the Unabomber.

The Trial

Kaczynski pleaded guilty. He was sentenced to four life terms plus 30 years. There is no possibility of parole.

He is in the "Supermax" prison near Colorado Springs, Colorado. That's the most secure federal prison in America. He will probably stay there for the rest of his life.

The Unabomber: Seventeen Years of Terror

May 25, 1978: A bomb explodes at Northwestern University. One person is hurt.

May 9, 1979: Another person is injured at Northwestern University.

Nov. 15, 1979: A bomb catches fire in the cargo area of an American Airlines plane. The plane makes an emergency landing. 12 people suffer smoke inhalation.

June 10, 1980: United Airlines president is hurt by a bomb at his home near Chicago.

Oct. 8, 1981: A bomb is found in a classroom at the University of Utah in Salt Lake City. No one is hurt.

May 5, 1982: One person is hurt at Vanderbilt University in Nashville, Tennessee.

July 2, 1982: A professor of electrical engineering and computer science is injured in the faculty lounge at University of California, Berkeley.

May 15, 1985: One person is injured by a bomb in a computer room at Berkeley.

June 13, 1985: A bomb mailed to Boeing Aircraft Co. in Auburn, Washington is safely disarmed.

Nov. 15, 1985: Two people are hurt by a bomb mailed to a professor at the University of Michigan at Ann Arbor.

Dec. 11, 1985: The first fatality: Sacramento, California, computer rental store owner Hugh Scrutton is killed when he picks up a bomb outside his store.

Feb. 20, 1987: The Unabomber is spotted. A witness in a Salt Lake City computer store sees a man in a hooded sweat shirt and sunglasses placing a bomb. Unabomber attacks halt for six years.

June 22, 1993: University of California, San Francisco geneticist Dr. Charles Epstein is injured by a bomb sent to his home.

June 24, 1993: Yale University computer expert David Gelernter is injured by a bomb in his office.

June 24, 1993: The Unabomber communicates for the first time in a letter to *The New York Times*.

Dec. 10, 1994: Advertising executive Thomas Mosser is killed when a bomb explodes at his New Jersey home.

April 24, 1995: The final bombing: the president of the California Forestry Association is killed opening a package in his Sacramento office.

Sept. 19, 1995: *The Washington Post* and *The New York Times* publish the Unabomber's 35,000-word manifesto, "Industrial Society and Its Future," following the serial bomber's promise to stop his attacks.

February 1996: David Kaczynski reads the manifesto and compares it to letters written by his brother, Ted. He calls the FBI.

April 3, 1996: Theodore Kaczynski is arrested at his mountain cabin in Montana.

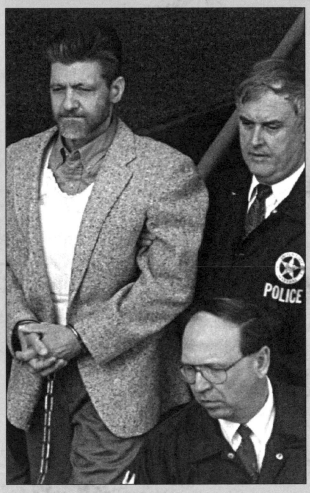

Confessed Unabomber Ted Kaczynski is now serving a life sentence in a high security federal prison in Colorado.

DATAFILE

Timeline

April 19, 1993

The FBI destroys a compound owned by the Branch Davidians, a religious cult that had been stockpiling guns. Many are killed.

April 19, 1995

The Murrah Building in Oklahoma City is destroyed by a bomb killing and injuring hundreds.

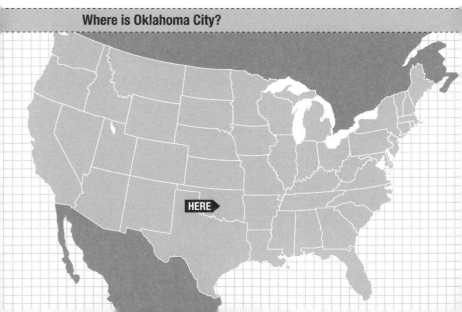

Where is Oklahoma City?

HERE

Key Terms

criminal record—a history of crimes that a
person has committed

execute—to put to death as legal punishment for
crimes the person committed

federal agents—people who work for the US
government

government building—a building where people
direct state or city affairs

CHAPTER 6 | Oklahoma City Bombing, 1995

It was the morning of April 19, 1995. A terrorist parked a truck filled with explosives. It was in front of a government building in Oklahoma City.

He walked away. A few minutes later, there was a huge explosion.

The blast shattered the building. Many people were killed instantly. Their bodies were blown apart.

Some of the dead were young children. They were playing in the building's day care center. It was right over the place where the truck was parked.

One side of the building crumbled to bits. The top floors collapsed. People were crushed. 168 died at the scene. Hundreds more were seriously injured.

The people of Oklahoma City were in shock. So were other Americans and people around the world. It was a terrorist attack. But who was responsible?

Many thought it was foreign terrorists. But the person behind this act of terrorism was American. He was twenty-six years old. His name was Timothy McVeigh.

McVeigh is Caught

Later that same day, a police officer saw an old car with no license plates. He stopped the car. It was about 75 miles from the scene of the attack.

The person driving the car had a gun. It was McVeigh. The officer was wary. He arrested McVeigh. The officer didn't know at the time that he had just arrested the Oklahoma City bomber.

McVeigh did not have a criminal record. He had never been arrested. Now, he was fingerprinted and photographed. And he was in jail.

Revenge

The FBI was on the case right after the bombing. They looked for terrorists from other countries. But someone noticed something special about the date of this attack. It was exactly two years after something had happened in Waco, Texas.

On February 28, 1993, police surrounded the home base of a group called the Branch Davidians. The Branch Davidians had lots of guns. They would not give up their guns.

For weeks, people waited to see what would happen. Timothy McVeigh went to Waco, Texas. He was on the side of the Branch Davidians. He wanted to see for himself what was going on.

On April 19, 1993, federal agents stormed the buildings where the Branch Davidians lived. There was shooting. Fires broke out. Many people died.

Timothy McVeigh saw what happened. He was furious. He thought the American government was wrong. He thought people should be allowed to have guns. He wanted revenge.

McVeigh did not act alone. He had some help from a friend named Terry Nichols. McVeigh and Nichols had been in the army together. Together they planned to blow up the Alfred P. Murrah building in Oklahoma City.

He and Nichols rented a truck. They filled it with explosives.

The FBI was right. The Oklahoma City bombing and the raid on the Branch Davidians were connected. McVeigh thought the agents who carried out the attack in Waco had offices in that building. He was wrong.

Many ordinary people worked in the building. McVeigh did not care who died. He would get his revenge, no matter who paid the price.

Guilty!

The police traced the truck back to McVeigh. There was a lot of evidence against him. Eventually, he admitted he had done it. The jury found him guilty. He was sentenced to death.

Timothy McVeigh was executed on June 11, 2001. Some of the victims' relatives watched him die.

McVeigh's death marked the end of this terrorist tragedy. But terrorism continued. And a worse terrorist disaster was yet to come.

DATAFILE

Timeline

January 2001

George W. Bush becomes the 43rd president of the United States.

September 11, 2001

Terrorists attack the World Trade Center in New York and the Pentagon in Washington, DC.

Where is New York?

HERE

Did You Know?

Osama bin Laden was the man behind the terror of 9/11. He was a wealthy man from Saudi Arabia.

Key Terms

Al-Qaeda—a group which opposes non-Islamic governments, often using violence

the Pentagon—headquarters of the Department of Defense

Twin Towers—two 110-story skyscrapers, together called the World Trade Center

CHAPTER 7 | September 11, 2001

On September 11, 2001, terrorists hijacked four planes. They crashed two of the jets into the Twin Towers of the World Trade Center in New York City.

Both towers caught fire and collapsed. Thousands of people inside were killed.

Some died when the airplanes hit the building. Some burned to death. Some jumped from windows. Others died when the buildings collapsed on top of them.

The third jet smashed into the Pentagon building. The fourth jet crashed in a field near Pittsburgh, Pennsylvania.

The terrorists planned to crash that plane into another target. But brave passengers on the plane stopped the terrorists. Everyone on all four planes died that day. It was the worst terrorist attack ever.

World Trade Center, New York City

The World Trade Center stood at the southern tip of Manhattan Island. The 110-story Twin Towers could be seen for miles.

They were a famous landmark. About 80,000 people visited the World Trade Center every day.

Another 50,000 people worked in the World Trade Center. There was a subway station at the World Trade Center. There were also shops and restaurants underground.

The Twin Towers were more than just huge office buildings. They were a symbol. They stood for the American way of life.

The terrorists chose to attack a place that meant America to everyone around the world. Their attack was brutal. Television images captured the horror.

The first plane smashed into the north tower at about 8:45 a.m. It tore a huge hole in the side of the building. The plane exploded.

The second slammed into the south tower about 15 minutes later. Both planes were full of jet fuel. The fuel burned. The fires were so hot that the steel beams in the buildings melted.

Many people escaped soon after the planes hit. But others on higher floors were trapped. Almost 3,000 people died at the World Trade Center that morning in September.

Hundreds of the victims were fire fighters and police. They had come to the scene to help. They were trying to save people when the towers fell.

New Yorkers were in shock. The city shut down. All the New York City airports were closed. Then all US flights were canceled.

Planes that were in the air had to land right away at the nearest airport. Flights from other countries were sent to Canada instead of the US. For the first time since jet travel began, there were no planes in the sky over America.

The landmark Twin Towers are no longer part of the New York landscape. On September 11, 2001, the towers collapsed after planes were crashed into each of the World Trade Center towers by terrorists

The Pentagon

As the Twin Towers burned, another hijacked plane crashed into the Pentagon. The Pentagon is the headquarters of the Department of Defense. It is in Arlington, Virginia. It contains offices for the military.

About 23,000 people work at the Pentagon. About 120 people who worked at the Pentagon were killed.

The Man Behind the Terror: Osama bin Laden

No terrorist group ever claimed responsibility for the attack. But there is little doubt who was behind the terror: Osama bin Laden.

Osama bin Laden was a wealthy Saudi Arabian. He was the head of a terrorist group called al-Qaeda ("the base"). They had killed American soldiers and blown up American embassies in other countries.

Al-Qaeda terrorists were also behind the 1993 bombing at the World Trade Center. That explosion killed six people. More than a thousand others were injured.

Firefighters battle flames and smoke after a plane hijacked by terrorists hits the Pentagon on September 11, 2001.

DATAFILE

Timeline

February 9, 1939

Two bombs explode at the King's Cross station of the London Underground.

July 7, 2005

After departing from the King's Cross Underground station, three trains are rocked by explosions that were detonated by suicide bombers.

Where is London, England?

HERE

Did You Know?

During rush hour, the most active part of the weekday morning commute, London's busiest Underground station is Waterloo, with 57,000 people entering. During the course of a year, 82 million passengers use Waterloo station.

Key Terms

celebratory—to observe a notable occasion with festivities

commuter rail—a passenger rail transport service between a city center and outer suburbs

suicide bomber—a terrorist who blows himself up in order to kill or injure other people

CHAPTER 8 | London Bombing

In the summer of 2005, the people of London were in a celebratory mood. The city had just won the right to host the 2012 Summer Olympic Games. There was pride among Londoners that they had won the Games over cities like New York and Paris.

The morning of July 7, 2005, was a typical day in London. Commuters were riding trains and buses into the city. London's subway system, the Underground, carries 3 million people each day. Officials estimated that about 500 trains were in use on July 7. Each train carried nearly 1,000 people.

It was the height of rush hour, around 8:50 in the morning. Three blasts detonated in the London Underground (also known as the Tube). Another bomb exploded later on the upper deck of a bus. The entire city of London erupted in chaos.

Timeline of Terror

The four bombers were spotted on security cameras at about 8:30 a.m. that morning. Each was wearing a backpack. The four traveled on a commuter train to the King's Cross station. King's Cross links the commuter rail lines to the Underground. They got off the train and spoke briefly to each other. Then they split up. Less than a half-hour later, three bombs went off.

At around 8:50 a.m., three bombs exploded. An Underground train near Aldgate Street was blown up. The train was waiting in the tunnel 100 yards away from the station. Metal doors were torn apart. Thick smoke filled the tunnels. Choking people stumbled, trying to escape to safety. Police and ambulances raced to the center of London. Eight people died in the bombing.

Another bomb exploded in the tunnel between King's Cross and Russell Square stations. All the trains were overflowing with passengers. A woman described hearing an "almighty bang." Inside the train cars, pieces of shattered glass flew into the passengers. The lights went out. Clouds of toxic smoke filled the cars.

The emergency lights in the tunnel kicked on. Survivors screamed and rushed out of the cars and onto the tracks. The driver shouted at people to stay off the tracks. The tracks might still be electrified.

Survivors stumbled up steps to the street. They were bleeding and choking from the smoke. Many were taken to ambulances and then to hospitals. The final death toll at King's Cross was 27.

Another explosion ripped through an Underground train arriving at Edgware Road. The explosion was powerful enough to blow holes in several nearby trains. Passengers were cut by flying glass and metal. Rescuers smashed windows and helped the injured out of twisted Tube cars.

The London Underground, commonly known as the Tube, is the oldest subway network in the world.

At first, the station manager at Edgware Road did not realize there had been an explosion. Then he saw passengers with bloodied faces running out of his station. The manager immediately called the police then helped the survivors. Seven people died in the Edgware Road explosion.

Above ground, the Number 30 double-decker bus moved slowly through London traffic. It had been almost an hour since the last Underground explosion. Many people could not use the Underground because of the bomb attacks. They were now trying to catch buses.

At approximately 9:47 a.m., the Number 30 bus stopped at the junction of Upper Woburn Place and Tavistock Square. Suddenly, the roof of the bus was ripped off by a fiery explosion. The explosion was so powerful that it threw large pieces of the metal roof ten feet in the air.

One survivor told of waiting for the Number 30. The bus had stopped and was letting off passengers. Then there was a huge explosion. "One minute the bus was there, the next it dissolved into millions of pieces," she said. "I tried to shield myself with my umbrella."

London intelligence officials believe the bus was not the planned target. The real target was another Underground station. But the bomber, Hasid Hussain, 18, was turned back from the Underground because the Northern Line station was closed. Fourteen people died in the Tavistock bombing.

Within a couple of hours, London's hospitals were full. Police said seriously injured people had lost limbs and were badly burned.

In the evening, London's streets were calm. Rail and Tube stations were closed. Thousands of people crowded the sidewalks trying to figure out how to get home. Some bomb survivors sat on curbs, dazed and covered in silver rescue blankets. The blankets helped the injured stay warm.

Not an Unexpected Attack

The British government had predicted a possible terrorist strike in London. Since the September 11 attacks in America, major cities around the world have been on alert.

The 2005 London Underground bombings killed 56 people, including the four bombers. More than 700 were injured, some very seriously. Al-Qaeda, the international terrorist organization, claimed responsibility for the bombings.

DATAFILE

Timeline

March 7, 1939

Civil war breaks out in Madrid between Communist and anti-Communist factions over control of Spain.

March 11, 2004

Suicide bombers detonate ten explosive devices on four commuter trains as they make their way into Madrid's Atocha station.

Where is Madrid, Spain?

HERE

Key Terms

detonate—explode or cause to explode

morgue—a place where bodies are kept, especially to be identified or claimed

shard—a piece of broken ceramic, metal, glass, or rock, typically having sharp edges

tourniquet—a device for stopping the flow of blood through an artery, typically by compressing a limb with a cord or tight bandage

CHAPTER 9 | Madrid Subway Bombing

On March 11, 2004, ten bombs were detonated on four commuter trains in Madrid. These bombs went off at almost the same time. Seven of the explosions were in or close to the Atocha station. This is the main train station in Madrid. It is usually crowded with Spaniards going to work and school. Many visiting tourists also use the Atocha station. The other three bombs went off in stations near Atocha.

Since the 9/11 attacks in America, many cities in Europe had been on high alert for terrorism. There had been warnings from the Spanish government about possible terrorist attacks in Spain. The subways and trains were thought to be major targets for terrorists.

The bombings happened only three days before an election in Spain. Police were already on the lookout for terrorism.

Rush Hour Terror

Around 6:45 on the morning of March 11, four trains entered the Alcala station on their way to Madrid. The trains left the Alcala station within 15 minutes of each other. As the trains stopped temporarily in Alcala, three men boarded the trains. The bombers ranged in age from 18 to 30. They loaded sports bags with explosives on the four trains. Each bag contained more than 20 pounds of powerful explosives.

Around 30 minutes later, the first train stopped inside Madrid's Atocha station. Just after 7:30 a.m., three huge bombs exploded. Several train cars were ripped apart by an explosion. At least 34 people were killed and dozens wounded.

At the same time, four more bombs exploded on a second train. At least 59 people were killed. Dozens more were wounded, many seriously.

This Metro sign in Madrid indicates that the Banco de España station is nearby.

Two more bombs exploded on a third train as it traveled to Madrid. At least 70 were killed and many wounded. One minute later, the fourth train passed through the Santa Eugenia station on its way to Madrid. A bomb exploded inside a single car. This bomb blast lifted the train off the tracks. The train almost broke in half.

The train was clouded in black smoke. Choking people pounded on windows to try to get air. Spanish paramedics pulled survivors through the windows to safety. Survivors told police they had been knocked over by a huge blast wave. The wave was so powerful that it blew some passengers through the roof of the train. Most of those passengers did not survive. More than 15 people were killed and dozens of others wounded.

Police quickly searched the Atocha station. They found two other unexploded bombs in backpacks. The police detonated them safely away from any people. Hours later, they found the final unexploded bomb with other luggage.

Madrid was in chaos. All trains into the city of Madrid were stopped. Police all over Madrid were worried that more bombs would go off.

Emergency crews set up a temporary hospital at a sports complex near the Atocha station. Police issued an order that commuter buses be used for ambulances. Each bus rushed dozens of injured to local hospitals. Other buses were used as temporary morgues for the dead.

Hundreds of injured survivors gathered around the Atocha station. Many were lying on the ground in shock. Passengers frantically called loved ones on their cell phones. But the lines were jammed by too many callers.

Rescue workers tried to save as many people as possible. They tied tourniquets on the legs and arms of survivors who had lost limbs. Hospitals reported running out of blood. The Spanish Red Cross put out an emergency call for blood. Local Spaniards lined up by the hundreds to donate.

Stories of Terror

At the Atocha station, a high school student said she was walking along the train platform with hundreds of others. Suddenly, there was a loud explosion. She was thrown to the ground, barely conscious. Smoke was everywhere. People were screaming for help. As the student ran for the exits, another explosion knocked her to the ground. She blacked out and woke up inside an ambulance.

The explosion that knocked out the student had hit one of the trains approaching the Atocha station. The train filled with smoke and flying glass. Passengers escaped through holes in the train.

A doctor going to work tried to help survivors. He wrapped bleeding wounds. He picked shards of glass out of people's skin. But he could not help everyone. Several lifeless bodies lay crumpled on the tracks. Their bodies were naked. The power of the explosion had burned their clothes off.

The Aftermath

The worst terrorist attack in Spanish history killed nearly 200 people. More than 1,800 were injured, some seriously.

A cell phone was discovered in one of the unexploded backpacks. The police traced the cell phone to people involved in the terrorist bombing. Several men were arrested. At least one had ties to the international terrorist organization al-Qaeda.

Spanish authorities searched all over the world for suspects. In Madrid, Spanish police were closing in on a group of the terrorists. They blew themselves up in their apartment. They were all killed. So was a Spanish policeman.

In October 2007, Spain's National Court convicted 21 men of the Madrid bombings. Seven others were found not guilty. Many Spaniards were upset that more suspects were not charged.

DATAFILE

Timeline

April 9, 1940

Near the start of World War II, Nazi German forces invade Norway, seizing control of the city of Oslo.

July 22, 2011

A car parked in front of the offices of Norway's prime minister explodes. Eight people are killed and over two hundred are injured.

Where is Norway?

HERE

Key Terms

fundamentalist—a supporter of a set of rigid principles with an intolerance of other views and opposition to secularism

hypothermia—rapid loss of body heat to a dangerously low temperature.

massacre—an indiscriminate and brutal slaughter of people

right-wing—the conservative or reactionary section of a political party or system

CHAPTER 10 | Oslo Killings

Utoya is a pretty island located in Tyrifjorden Lake in Norway. It is about one hour's drive north of Oslo. It is less than 30 acres in size and is heavily covered with pine trees. A ferry takes visitors to and from the island.

Every year, Norway's Labor Party holds a summer camp for young people who are interested in politics. It is a popular camp attended by hundreds of people. Most of them are under 20 years old.

A Bomb Explodes

It was Friday, July 22, 2011, at around 3:30 in the afternoon. A huge blast shook the city center of Oslo. The sound of the explosion could be heard more than a mile away. Glass and debris covered the streets of Oslo. The offices of Norway's Prime Minister and other government buildings were severely damaged. One building had every window blown out.

Norwegian police officers arrived quickly. They helped survivors who staggered out of buildings covered in blood. Dozens of injured people were taken to hospitals. Eight people were confirmed dead. Fortunately, many Norwegians were out of town on vacation. Many more people could have died.

A Deadly Preview

Anders Behring Breivik, 32, is a Norwegian man. Police described him as a body-builder and right-wing Christian fundamentalist. Breivik posted messages on the Internet saying he wanted to keep Muslims out of Norway.

It was Breivik who planted the car bomb in Oslo. He used the bombing as a distraction for what he had planned next. While police were busy dealing with the Oslo bombing, Breivik drove to the ferry that would take him to Utoya. He was disguised as a policeman.

At the landing, Breivik showed a fake police identification card. It was good enough to trick security guards. They let Breivik get on the ferry boat for the short trip to Utoya. It was now almost 5:00 p.m. Less than two hours had gone by since the Oslo bombings.

Still dressed as a police officer, Breivik arrived at the island. He carried a machine gun and pistol. There were hundreds of summer campers on the island, most of them teenagers. The campers had just heard about the Oslo bombing. They gathered together to talk and support each other.

Breivik walked up to a large group of young campers. He told everyone he was a policeman and was there to protect them. He instructed the campers to go to the main building on the island. Inside, they would be able to watch the news about the Oslo bombing. Then Breivik put on earplugs.

Dozens of campers crowded into the main lodge. Breivik was outside, encouraging everyone to go in. Quickly, the lodge filled up. Then Breivik rushed inside the house and started shooting people.

The campers ran from the house screaming and bleeding. Others were dead already. One survivor told police she and her friends hid in a bathroom. They locked the door and lay down on the floor. Outside, they could hear shooting and their friends' screams.

Breivik chased the campers down one by one. He pursued his victims down to the water and into caves. Campers were hit by bullets as they climbed rocks to escape. One fell from the rocks and died. Other campers ran to the chilly waters and jumped in. They swam for their lives. One person drowned. Others were shot by Breivik as they swam.

Local residents used their boats to pick up some of the swimmers. But many of the boats were small and could not take everyone. Breivik stood on shore shooting at people in the water. He shot at people in trees. Breivik laughed and cheered himself as he killed people. He was heard to say, "You all must die." Some victims were as young as 14.

Finally, Norwegian police arrived on the island. It had taken them more than an hour since the first reports of shooting on Utoya. Many Norwegians later criticized the slow response.

Police and medical workers immediately started helping the injured. Many campers had multiple gunshot wounds and were bleeding heavily. Others were suffering from shock and hypothermia from swimming in the cold lake.

The surviving campers pointed police to the area where Breivik was still shooting. At first, the campers were afraid to meet the police, since Breivik had disguised himself as a policeman.

The Norwegian police spread out, aiming their weapons toward the forest. As police entered the forest, they found Breivik standing alone. He put his hands above his head and surrendered. Breivik still had large amounts of ammunition left. The Utoya shootings were over. The horrible events lasted an hour and a half.

People gather in mourning outside the Oslo Cathedral in downtown Oslo after two terror attacks hit Norway.

Eight people died in the Oslo bombing. More than 200 were injured. At Utoya, the death toll was 69. More than 100 were injured. The bombing and shootings were the worst massacre in Norway's modern history.

Glossary

brainwash—to change a person's beliefs by force

celebratory—to observe a notable occasion with festivities

commuter rail—a passenger rail transport service between a city center and outer suburbs

criminal record—a history of crimes that a person has committed

detonate—explode or cause to explode

execute—to put to death as legal punishment for crimes the person committed

executive—a person who manages or administers a business or school, etc.

federal agents—people who work for the US government

fundamentalist—a supporter of a set of rigid principles with an intolerance of other views and opposition to secularism

government—a system of political control by which a nation is governed.

government building—a building where people direct state or city affairs

grenade—a small bomb often thrown by hand

hijack—to take control of a car, bus, plane, or train, etc., by force

hostage—a person held against his or her will by a terrorist

hypothermia—rapid loss of body heat to a dangerously low temperature.

investigate—to search systematically in order to learn the facts

massacre—an indiscriminate and brutal slaughter of people

mastermind—a clever person who plans and directs a group project

morgue—a place where bodies are kept, especially to be identified or claimed

pardon—to free someone from further punishment

parole—the freedom granted to a prisoner for future good behavior

the Pentagon—headquarters of the Department of Defense

right-wing—the conservative or reactionary section of a political party or system

shard—a piece of broken ceramic, metal, glass, or rock, typically having sharp edges

suicide bomber—a terrorist who blows himself up in order to kill or injure other people

terrorism—using force or threats against people

tourniquet—a device for stopping the flow of blood through an artery, typically by compressing a limb with a cord or tight bandage

Index